No Horses in the House!

The Audacious Life of Artist Rosa Bonheur

Story by
Mireille Messier

Illustrations by
Anna Bron

ORCA BOOK PUBLISHERS

France, 1829

Once there was a girl named Rosa who loved to draw animals.

Every morning she put on her bloomers, petticoat and dress and headed outside to draw. She drew cats and dogs, goats and cows, rabbits and ducks. But what she most loved to draw was horses. Rosa could draw horses all day long.

"You must learn to read!" said her mother.
"But Maman, I just want to draw!"
So her mother devised a clever game. Rosa would learn to read by drawing an animal for each letter of the alphabet. It worked.

As Rosa grew older, she kept on drawing.
"You must learn to sew!" said her father.
"No, Papa, I just want to draw."
Many teachers tried to show Rosa how to sew, embroider, cook and garden—the things other girls her age did. This did not go well.

Eventually her father agreed to teach Rosa how to draw, paint and sculpt at home, like her brothers. This went much better!

But the family's neighbors and friends didn't approve of how Rosa was spending her days.

They frowned and said, "You can't be an artist!"

"Why not?" Rosa asked.

"Because you are a girl."

Rosa did not agree—she would be an artist. The first girl to be an artist on her street...in her arrondissement...in all of Paris even. And she would be the best one they had ever seen.

Rosa studied animals, drawing them day and night. Their eyes. Their fur. Their muscles. Their feathers. Every pen and paintbrush stroke took her work closer to perfection.

One day, while scouting the city for new animals to draw, Rosa discovered the horse market. Here, in this messy, smelly place, she found many fascinating breeds of horses. Some were breeds Rosa had never seen before. She was thrilled.

"Hey! Girls can't be in the market!" snarled a merchant. "It's too dangerous."

"It's unladylike!" sneered another.

"You'll make a mess of your dress," added his friend.

"Balivernes!" cried Rosa. "Nonsense!"

Despite her protests, the merchants dragged her away, warning her not to return.

Rosa stayed home, but she missed the horses. Without them, how could she paint eyes that looked like real eyes? And a mane that flowed like a real mane? She needed to sketch from life.

So she made do with other, smaller animals. Bit by bit, Rosa filled her family's apartment with dogs...cats...birds... rabbits...ducks. One day she even brought home a goat.

But what Rosa really wanted was a horse.
"No horses in the house!" warned her father.

"If the horses can't come to me, then I will go to the horses!" Rosa hissed. She dressed in her brother's clothing, grabbed her paintbrushes and slipped off to the market.

Nobody noticed the young "boy" quietly sketching in a shadowy corner. Until...

"YOU AGAIN? Girls CANNOT dress like boys!" said the policeman.

"This is against the law! Out!"

"What about them?" Rosa pointed. "Why can these men dress like women?"

"They have a special permission from the police."

"Then I will get a special permission too!"

The policeman laughed. "Such a permit has never been given to a girl," he said.

"Balivernes!"

It wasn't easy, but Rosa petitioned and pleaded and pressed. A few weeks later she returned to the horse market with her paintbrushes in her hand...and a special permit allowing her to dress any way she wanted. Now no one could stop her.

When Rosa exhibited her paintings for the first time at the prestigious Salon de Paris, people rushed to see the work of this peculiar pant-wearing, animal-loving, rule-defying young lady.

"They are so lifelike!"

"Look at those eyes!"

"I can almost see the animals breathe!"

But she had not changed everyone's mind.

"Pfft! She never even went to art school."

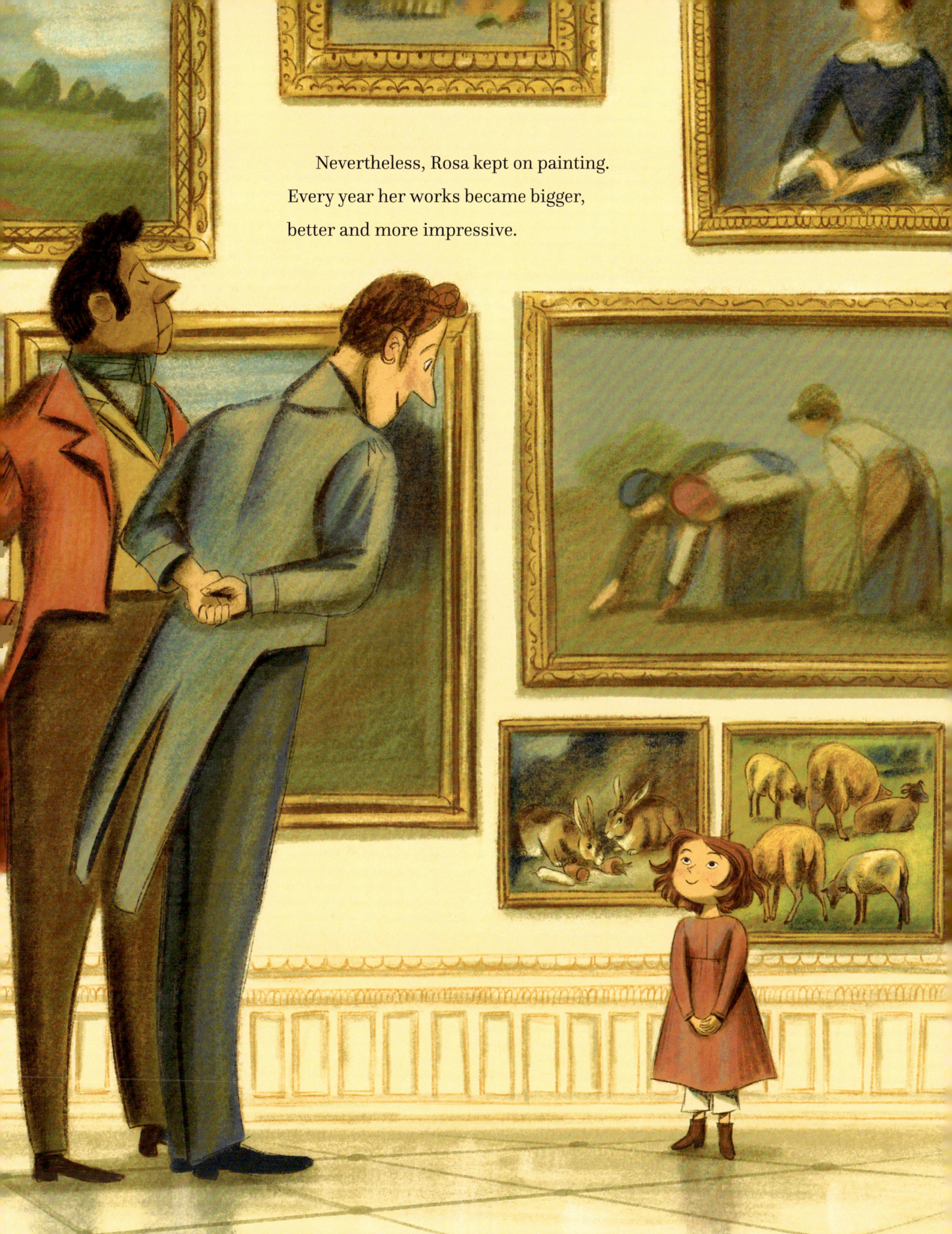

Nevertheless, Rosa kept on painting. Every year her works became bigger, better and more impressive.

Then, one year, her newest painting was so beautiful that kings and queens came from faraway lands to see it.
"Introducing *The Horse Fair*, by Rosa Bonheur!"
Art lovers were in awe.
"Magnifique!"
"Stunning!"
"Splendid!"

And the girl who loved to draw animals became one of the most famous artists in France.

Author's Note

Rosa Bonheur's life was far from picture perfect. She was a girl who loved and created art at a time when her gender dictated that she could not be an artist.

Luckily, Rosa Bonheur was also stubborn as a mule!

Because she was a girl, she was denied a formal art education, and she wasn't allowed to go where she wanted or dress how she pleased. And when her paintings were exhibited, other artists belittled her work. Yet she remained determined and lived her life on her own terms.

After many twists and turns, Rosa became the most famous female artist of her day!

Sadly, Rosa Bonheur's art style, realism, fell out of fashion after she died, and Rosa's legacy was largely forgotten.

Rosa's masterpieces are still in museums across the world today, just waiting to inspire a new generation of rule-defying artists!

Rosa Bonheur Milestones

1822 — Marie-Rosalie (Rosa) Bonheur is born in Bordeaux, France.

1829 — Rosa and her family move to Paris.

1833 — Rosa is expelled from many schools for her "unruliness."

1837 — Rosa meets Nathalie Micas, and they become inseparable.

1841 — Rosa exhibits *Rabbits Nibbling Carrots* and *Goats and Sheep* at the Salon de Paris.

1845 — Rosa exhibits six paintings at the Salon de Paris and wins the third-place medal.

1848 — Rosa wins the gold medal at the Salon.

1849 — The French government commissions Rosa to paint a bucolic scene.

1850 — Rosa becomes the director of a free art school for girls and enlists her sister Juliette to help.

1851 — Rosa starts dressing like a boy to sneak into markets.

1852 — Rosa gets a special permit from the police to wear trousers.

1853 — Rosa completes *The Horse Fair*—the painting is twice her height!

1857 — Fellow artist Édouard Louis Dubufe paints a portrait of Rosa standing by a table. With his permission, she paints over the table and makes it a bull.

1859 — Rosa buys a château in By and turns it into a huge studio and menagerie.

1865 — Rosa is the first woman artist to receive the Legion of Honor in France.

1889 — Nathalie Micas, Rosa's lifelong partner, dies.

1889 — Rosa meets and becomes friends with Buffalo Bill.

1899 — Rosa dies at her château in Thomery, France.

For my mother, Jeanne, who took me to the Louvre and taught me to love art.
—M.M.

For Nancy Crawford, Julia Bennett and Peter Sarganis,
the most brilliant art teachers.
—A.B.

Text copyright © Mireille Messier 2023
Illustrations copyright © Anna Bron 2023

Published in Canada and the United States in 2023 by Orca Book Publishers.
orcabook.com

All rights reserved. No part of this publication may be reproduced or transmitted in any form or by any means, electronic or mechanical, including photocopying, recording or by any information storage and retrieval system now known or to be invented, without permission in writing from the publisher.

Library and Archives Canada Cataloguing in Publication

Title: No horses in the house! : the audacious life of artist Rosa Bonheur / Mireille Messier ; illustrated by Anna Bron.
Names: Messier, Mireille, 1971- author. | Bron, Anna, 1989- illustrator.
Description: Issued also in French under title:
Pas de chevaux dans la maison! : la vie audacieuse de l'artiste Rosa Bonheur.
Identifiers: Canadiana (print) 20220199426 | Canadiana (ebook) 20220199566 | ISBN 9781459833524 (hardcover) | ISBN 9781459833531 (PDF) | ISBN 9781459833548 (EPUB)
Subjects: LCSH: Bonheur, Rosa, 1822-1899—Juvenile literature. | LCSH: Women painters—France—Biography—Juvenile literature. | LCSH: Animal painters—France—Biography—Juvenile literature.
Classification: LCC ND553.B6 M47 2023 | DDC j759.4—dc23

Library of Congress Control Number: 2022935248

Summary: A delightful picture book based on the true story of Rosa Bonheur, the nineteenth-century French artist who defied gender expectations and changed the art world with her realistic animal paintings.

Orca Book Publishers is committed to reducing the consumption of nonrenewable resources in the production of our books. We make every effort to use materials that support a sustainable future.

Orca Book Publishers gratefully acknowledges the support for its publishing programs provided by the following agencies: the Government of Canada, the Canada Council for the Arts and the Province of British Columbia through the BC Arts Council and the Book Publishing Tax Credit.

Cover and interior artwork by Anna Bron
Design by Rachel Page and Anna Bron

Interior paintings on pp. 30 and 31, respectively:
Rosa Bonheur in Her Atelier (1893). Painting by Georges Achille-Fould. George Achille-Fould/Wikimedia Commons/Public Domain.
Gathering for the Hunt (1856). Painting by Rosa Bonheur, Haggin Museum, Stockton, CA. Rosa Bonheur/Wikimedia Commons/Public Domain.

Printed and bound in Canada.

26 25 24 23 • 1 2 3 4